Three Steps Ahead

Other books by David Silverstein:

Become an Elite Mental Athlete

One Dot, Two Dots, Get Some New Dots

What's Good for the Goose Could Cook the Gander

The Innovator's Toolkit: 50+ Techniques for Predictable and Sustainable Organic Growth

Insourcing Innovation: How to Transform Business as Usual Into Business as Exceptional

THREE STEPS AHEAD

AHEAD

Thinking strategically to avoid unintended consequences

By David Silverstein

Three Steps Ahead

by David Silverstein

Published by Breakthrough Performance Press
1200 17th Ave., Suite 180
Denver, CO 80202

Editor: Jessica Harper
Designer: Rob Herman
Illustrators: Josh Abraham, Brian Miller

ISBN-13: 978-1-938353-04-8

Printed in the United States of America

Contents

Contents •

Game theory is a way to think about choices—your choices and the choices made by others in reaction to the choices you might make.

PART 3: What To Do About It

The way to minimize the negative impact of unintended consequences—or to maximize their opportunity—is to think through the possibilities.

Positive consequences can be gained from thinking about all of the negative things that can go wrong.

A stoic management philosophy helps you identify what you can't control so you focus on what you can do something about.

Scenario planning, and its little brother what-if analysis, are excellent strategic thinking tools that are well suited for anticipating (and avoiding) unexpected consequences.

We're much more likely to anticipate the possibility of unintended consequences if we use a systems thinking approach of seeing interrelationships and patterns.

Contents

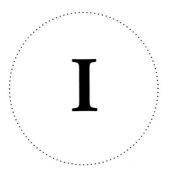

WHY UNINTENDED CONSEQUENCES MATTER

Grandma loved to play cards—and so did I. Gin rummy was her game, but the first game she taught me was war. If you've ever played war, it's a very fun game for a 4-year old. The rules are easy to understand and anyone can win. It's a pure game of chance.

Tic-tac-toe? It's not war, but it's still very fast and easy to teach. It's another great game for young kids.

Checkers gets a little more complicated, but it can still be learned—even mastered—at a pretty early age. All the pieces are alike. They all move the same way. And what could be more fun than "jumping" other pieces? While seemingly simple, checkers is certainly not purely a game of chance.

Then there's chess. My father taught me to play chess. Chess is complicated. The pieces are different; they move differently; and at a young age chess just seems to cause headaches. I can't say I had the patience necessary when I first started learning, but over time, I learned.

My father really enjoys teaching—whether it's teaching a young boy to play chess or my mother to play golf in retirement, my father is always instructing. And I remember when he was teaching me chess…he would constantly ask, "Ok, so what do you think I'm going to do next?"

At the age of 5 your first answer is, "I don't know and I don't care. This is where I want to move." But after being asked time and time again, you start to learn that chess is all about thinking ahead—and the player that can think more moves ahead than his opponent wins. In chess you cannot win without thinking ahead—it's that simple.

I'd like to do a quick exercise here. Get yourself a pen or pencil and actually write down your answers before reading on.

Rank the following games in order from easiest to hardest. Write 1 next to the game that is the easiest and then 2, 3, and 4, with 4 being the hardest game.

Checkers	_____
War	_____
Chess	_____
Tic-tac-toe	_____

Now here are MY answers.

Checkers	2
War	4 (hardest)
Chess	1 (easiest)
Tic-tac-toe	3

Confused? Let's go back to the question: Which game is the easiest? What, exactly, does "easy" mean? If you labeled war as the easiest, with tic-tac-toe second, checkers third and chess fourth, you're not alone. That's how nine out of 10 people answer—because they're answering the question, "the easiest to learn" or "understand."

But in the end, game playing is about winning and losing and of the four, chess is the easiest game to win.

In a game of war, no matter what I do (unless I cheat), I have a 50/50 chance of winning. No better. No worse. And nothing I can do about it. Charge me with "winning" in war and I'm left helpless.

In tic-tac-toe, even a modestly competent opponent can force me to a draw every time. You can't win tic-tac-toe when both competitors know how to play. At best you hope for the other to make a mistake and through some diligence, you might get the slightest of edge. That makes it a game of endurance, I suppose. But again, charge me with "winning," and I'm still pretty helpless.

Checkers is actually a more complicated game than it seems. The rules are very easy to learn, but the strategy is not as simple as it seems. Position and forcing your opponent to take pieces when they don't want to is the key. In checkers you have to think several moves ahead to be truly competitive. The person who studies and practices at checkers has a real advantage, but your opponent can do the same, which can quickly negate your advantage. Your ability to work hard, study, and practice is certainly greater than in war or tic-tac-toe, but developing a sustainable competitive advantage at checkers is still very hard.

Chess is by far the most challenging game to learn. Chess strategy can get very complicated, but all great chess players eventually learn the same strategies. The winners are those who can see the greatest number of permutations on the board—combinations of moves and countermoves. It's said that a grand-master is often looking 10 or more moves out. In reality it's more complicated than that. In some cases the number of possibly good moves is so numerous that they can see only four or five moves out. Other times it can be many more than 10. But 10 is a good reference point.

Chess, then, has the greatest opportunity for exploitation. Learning the many strategies takes far more time and effort than learning war, checkers, or tic-tac-toe strategies. Practice, practice, practice—and more practice—to learn to "see" the whole board, to think many moves and countermoves ahead, gives the serious chess player a much greater opportunity to dominate his opponent than in any other game.

So if you ask me the easiest game to win—the one that I would bank on the most with the least left to chance and the most given to the results of my efforts—I would choose chess every time because if you train yourself to think ahead, you will likely come out ahead, just like in life and business. It's that concept that has compelled me to write this book.

Thinking three steps ahead as you formulate a strategy can not only help propel you forward, but also avoid dangerous pitfalls along the way.

***

In the predawn hours of a chilly January morning, five million residents of Kobe, Japan, awoke in terror as the ground shifted violently beneath them. A major fault deep under an island in Kobe Bay had shifted, causing a 20-second earthquake that ruptured gas lines, broke electrical lines, and set more than 150 fires ablaze across the city.[1] In all, the quake killed almost 6,000 people, injured more than 30,000, and rendered 300,000 homeless. Many of the injured made their way to Kobe's hospitals. Yet 85 percent of these hospitals had also suffered damage from the earthquake and sustained a combined

$1 billion in damage. Moreover, the lack of running water, gas, and electricity hampered medical care even at the healthcare facilities that were not directly damaged by the quake.

The Japanese government rushed to aid people, filling the massive health-care gap by establishing free health clinics to help the injured. But this aid-giving had an unintended consequence. Ironically, it proved too successful by staying operational for too long. As a consequence, it almost bankrupted most of Kobe's hospitals, which couldn't compete with free care. A well-intentioned government intervention caused secondary damage.

The Kobe story is an example of an unintended consequence. Simply put, *unintended consequences* are the unexpected outcomes of purposeful action that are contrary or divergent from the expected outcome. They're unforeseen and unanticipated. In many cases, they are negative, like the example above, but they can be positive, too. For example, aspirin was engineered to be a pain reliever but can also reduce the risk of heart attacks and stroke, which is a positive but unintended benefit.[2]

In many cases, unintended consequences are not foreseen or predicted because no one took the time to try to foresee or predict them. My goal for this book is to help you think more strategically, to help you connect the dots so you can anticipate consequences better.

When talking of strategy, academics and consultants put forth dozens of definitions that I won't bore you with other than to tell you they all have one simple thing in common: Strategy is about intention. It's about making something happen. That something can be winning a football game or making it to the Super Bowl (or World Cup for my non-American readers); it can mean winning market share in a competitive industry; or it can mean curing a disease. In each case, the purpose of strategy is to make something happen intentionally. Thus you can consider unintended consequences to be the result of a strategic faux pas. When unintended things happen, our strategy was flawed.

Now, you might argue with me and say that there are some things that you simply cannot foresee. And you're right. But in such a case, your strategy should acknowledge the degree of unknown and the risk associated with it, and provide alternatives, mitigation, or protection from unintended consequences. When strategy is well-designed and comprehensive, unintended consequences should be of little consequence.

In the coming chapters, I'll explain the causes of unintended consequences, why they happen, and what you can do to anticipate them.

Part 1 of this book comprises four chapters that explain why unintended consequences happen. Knowing these patterns will [hopefully] prompt you to be on the lookout for when one of these forces is in play. In Part 2, I'll provide you with ways to estimate the likelihood of what can go awry. We humans are notoriously bad at thinking in terms of probability and statistics, which contributes to our getting bitten by consequences. Part 3 focuses on action. Just because something bad *can* happen doesn't mean it will happen, nor does it mean we can't take action. Each of the chapters in Part 3 describes a specific tool or technique for anticipating and managing unintended consequences.

Finally, I want to stress that the potential presence of unintended consequences should not be used to rule out an action. A given action might well produce some negative consequences, or collateral damage. But it might also deliver enough positive consequences that it justifies the risks or side effects.

Instead of justifying inaction, this book will help decision makers take better actions in three ways. First, the book will help you avoid nasty surprises that negate the benefits of your action. Second, it will help you understand the impact of your choices and balance the various positive and negative consequences. Third, by foreseeing unintended consequences, you can mitigate them before they occur.

Overall, this book will describe tools and ways of thinking to help you stay three steps ahead.

Part 1

Why Unintended Consequences Happen

1

COMPLEX SYSTEMS

In the early 1980s, the Philippine government wanted to augment the food supply of its poorest farmers. The farmers subsisted on rice, supplementing it by eating the small black snails that lived in the rice fields all over the Philippines. Unfortunately, the number of available snails was diminishing with the use of pesticides. So, in 1983, the government introduced the Golden Apple Snail. This snail could grow quickly to the size of an apple, and its creamy flesh was lauded by Manila's top chefs. The snail would add protein to farmers' diets and could be exported to Europe and the U.S. to satisfy demand for escargot.

But the Golden Apple Snail held a dark secret inside its spiral shell. Each female snail could lay up to 15,000 eggs, and each egg could hatch and mature in 60 days. The snails got into the rice paddies, multiplied prodigiously, and ate most of the rice crop. Instead of supplementing the farmer's food, the snails ate the farmer's food. By 1989, Golden Apple Snails had destroyed 15 percent of the country's total rice crop, and in some areas as much as 75 percent of the crop was destroyed. To this day, the government is struggling to eradicate this invasive pest.[3]

Unintended consequences like these happen because we live in a complex, interconnected world. Taking one action can cause an unintended reaction if we don't think through—or even dare to imagine—the possibilities.

Systems Thinking Reveals Interconnections

What are the forces that strike—the forces that cause these unintended consequences? Systems thinking provides us with a clue. Systems thinking is a way of looking at the world as one big system made up of countless interconnected smaller systems.[4] All of these parts can be linked via various positive, negative, and nonlinear effects that can lead to unintended consequences.

I'll describe systems thinking in more detail in Chapter 12, but here's a quick introduction to these three effects.

"Doesn't that breeze feel great?"

The Unintended Mute Button

First, there's negative feedback. A *negative feedback loop* mutes an effect we were expecting. For example, to decrease air pollution in Beijing, officials mandated drivers could only drive a maximum of six days a week. The mandate reduced traffic congestion and increased the average driving speed, which inadvertently led to increases in particulate emissions, according to researchers at Tsinghua University in China.[5] As a result, the directive did little to improve air quality, and may have even had a negative impact on it.

Mexico City tried a slightly different program designed to lower emissions, with an equally unsuccessful result. The government banned drivers from using their car one day a week based on the last number of their license plate. To get around the ban, people bought used cars, with different ending numbers on the registration plate. Drivers ended up driving their newer, lower emission cars one day and higher-emitting beaters the next. The net result was no effect at all.[6]

Often, human resistance to change dampens the effect of change because humans take action to suppress it. As in physics, every action generates a reaction.

A Runaway Success (or Failure)

Second, whereas negative feedback mutes a big effect, a *positive feedback loop* amplifies a tiny effect we were expecting. Groupthink, crowd mentality, and something going viral are all examples of positive feedback loops. As the Grumpy Cat Internet phenomenon demonstrates, one photo of a scowling cat can turn into a business empire of T-shirts, books, calendars, and media appearances.[7]

It's important to note that positive feedback loops don't imply the result is positive or desirable, but rather amplified. An example of a positive feedback loop can be seen when polar ice caps melt. As temperatures rise, ice melts, exposing more dark land or seawater to the hot sun. Land and seawater absorb more solar radiation than bright white ice, thus further raising ambient temperatures, causing the ice to melt faster, absorbing more solar radiation, and so forth.

Delayed Reactions

Some things are proportionally linked to each other and result in nonlinear effects. Turn the knob up on a stove, and more heat pours out of the burner or coil. But other parts of a system can make an impact that is not immediately noticeable. For example, turning up the heat on the stove doesn't make the pot of water instantly and proportionally hotter. Instead, it takes time for the heat to accumulate. Turn off the stove, and the heated pot stays hot for a long time. Like a tea kettle of water, unintended consequences can take time to accumulate and may be slow to disappear.

Similarly, we all know people who over-adjust the thermostat. If the room is cold, they turn it up. If the room is really cold, they turn it up even more. But setting the thermostat to 90 won't make the room get warmer any faster; it will just cause the temperature in the room to overshoot a comfortable temperature.

A Straw That Breaks the Camel's Back

You may have noticed that heating soup in the microwave for three minutes makes a nice hot bowl of soup, but heating it for three-and-a-half minutes makes a boiled-over mess. Some systems have *nonlinear or threshold effects,* in which a given action might have a modest effect for some time but then suddenly changes to have a much larger, unintended impact. Examples of this include phase changes, such as when liquid water turns to gaseous steam, or when free-flowing highway traffic turns into a congested snarl. Likewise, the proper dose of medicine can cure patients, but an overdose of that same medicine might kill them.

Finally, human nature is a big culprit in unintended consequences. As we'll see in Chapter 4: Contrary Reactions, people will always try to game the system, thereby mitigating the effects being targeted by the key players.

2

MERTON'S 5 CAUSES OF
UNINTENDED CONSEQUENCES

In Chapter 1, I explained the systems view of how different dynamics can cause unintended consequences. The characteristics of systems are like natural laws: They operate independently of human behavior. But we humans are the primary actors on earth—the actions we take are the ones most likely to cause an unintended consequence. For this reason, it's useful to look at unintended consequences through the lens of sociology.

Robert K. Merton, an American sociologist living in the 1930s, identified five factors that lead to unanticipated consequences:
      1. Ignorance
      2. Error
      3. Immediate interest
      4. Basic values
      5. Self-defeating prophecy [8] [9]

Let's look at each of these factors in turn.

The More You Know…

First, by "ignorance," Merton means a lack of knowledge about what might happen. Sometimes, we simply don't have enough information to know the full consequences of our actions. I live in Boulder, Colo., and saw this "ignorance" as I watched flames from the Sugarloaf fire engulf friends' homes. Early in the 20th century, the U.S. government suppressed fires in national forests to preserve timber, an important natural resource. The U.S. Forest Service was allowed unlimited spending to quell a fire. The "10 a.m. policy" enacted in 1935 advocated suppressing any fire by 10 a.m. the day after it was discovered.[10]

It wasn't until the 1970s that ecologists realized the policy actually increased the likelihood and severity of wildfires. Fire suppression resulted in dead leaves, branches, and trees accumulating in forests, waiting for a spark, lightning strike, or careless camper's fire. Then when a fire did start, the abundant fuel created a hot conflagration reaching the crowns of trees and jumping from tree-top to tree-top, consuming everything in its path. The more we suppress forest fires, the more fuel that builds up, and thus the bigger the future fire.

It Looks the Same, But Is It the Same?

The second cause of unintended consequences is "error": having some information but making a mistake in the analysis of the problem at hand. We might think that what worked in the past or worked elsewhere will work again, but perhaps the conditions changed during the intervening time, or the two situations are different. By not taking those changes or differences into account, we run into unintended consequences.

For example, in the 1930s, beetles were a problem for Australian sugar cane growers. The government looked for solutions and found that sugar cane farms in Hawaii had faced a similar problem; however, cane toads in Hawaii were eating the beetles and thereby reducing the damage. In 1935, the Australians imported 100 cane toads, assuming the toads would improve sugar cane yields Down Under.

But both the beetles and the cane fields were different in Australia compared to Hawaii. Australian cane fields were plagued by the greenback beetle, which lives at the tops of sugar cane stalks, six to eight feet off the ground. The breed of cane toads the government imported couldn't reach the beetles. Being unable to eat most of the beetles, the toads offered minimal benefit to the crop yields.

Worse, Australia's sugar cane fields are drier than those in Hawaii, and cane toads prefer moisture. So, the cane toads started migrating from the fields. Cane toads eat just about anything that fits in their mouths: small lizards, snakes, frogs, tadpoles, marsupials, mice, and terrestrial and aquatic insects. What's more, the toads' poisonous skins killed any predators who tried to eat them, thus killing native Australian species.

The cane toads multiplied rapidly, and Australia now has more than 200 million cane toads that continue to spread out into the continent, destroying native species. Cane toads are now one of the country's biggest environmental blunders and the government is trying to mount a response. [11][12][13]

A Quick Fix Now, But…

The third cause of unanticipated consequences, "immediate interest," refers to immediate needs overriding consideration of longer-term interests. Sometimes, people want the intended consequence of an action so much that they purposefully ignore any long-term unintended effects. I'll talk more about this topic in Chapter 3.

The Spirit Moves Us (in the Wrong Direction)

Fourth, "basic values" may compel us to act or not act in certain ways, even if the long-term result of those actions might be detrimental.

In 1830s Ireland, a priest named Theobald Mathew led a temperance movement in which three million followers vowed never to drink alcohol again. The followers didn't vow not to consume other intoxicants though, so when given the opportunity to consume diethyl ether, many of them succumbed.

Diethyl ether is a much more dangerous intoxicant than alcohol, and it is highly flammable. Many imbibers died in fires when the ether vapors ignited due to burning candles. An estimated 50,000 people drank 17,000 gallons of diethyl ether.[14][15][16] Strictly speaking, the followers weren't breaking their pledge, but the outcomes of imbibing diethyl ether rather than alcohol were worse.

So Likely (and Feared) That It Does Not Happen

Finally, the fifth factor leading to unanticipated consequences, "self-defeating prophecy" refers to people taking action before a problem occurs and through that action causing the original problem not to occur at all, which is unanticipated. Warnings early in the 20th century that population growth would lead to mass starvation resulted in a self-defeating prophecy when it spurred scientific breakthroughs in agricultural productivity that have since made it unlikely that the gloomy prophecy will come true.[17] Another example: "Peak Oil" has been happening for decades and yet the motivation to uncover new oil reserves or further extract trapped oil and gas implies that oil production continues to grow.

As you can see, unintended consequences occur more often due to human behaviors rather than natural circumstances. Let's look more closely at why this happens.

3

THE HUMAN BIAS FOR ACTION (AND INACTION)

People love to fix things, even if they aren't broken and even if the cure is worse than the disease. The human bias for choosing action over inaction is a major driver of unintended consequences. Consider that modern man appeared only 100,000 years ago, a blink of the eye in our planet's history. Somehow, planet earth managed to survive for 4.5 billion years without the help of man. Nature has many built-in mechanisms to correct problems. Negative feedback loops (such as predators, germs, and the evolution of clever prey) all conspire to keep the positive feedback loop of a species' rampant reproduction in check.

"No thanks — I prefer my glass half full."

But humans are an impatient species, and our bias toward action often yields unintended results. This is evident in many things—from our attempts to manage the environment to economics. A big question is whether we are executing on emotionally driven and short-sighted opinions or on detailed strategic analysis. All too often, it is the former.

Cheap Food Causes Starvation

If we see people starving, we want to send them food. When Bill Clinton was U.S. president, he helped bring inexpensive food, specifically rice, to the people of impoverished Haiti by subsidizing U.S. farmers and supporting a reduction in Haiti's import tariffs.[18] But the plan did not work as intended.

By bringing in outside food for cheap-to-nonexistent prices, Clinton unintentionally drove local rice farms out of business. Compounded by natural disasters and aid efforts, the formerly agricultural country now imports half of its food and 80 percent of its rice.[19] The unintentional outcome of Clinton's actions was calamitous resulting in even higher levels of poverty and food insecurity. He recently said, "I have to live every day with the consequences of the lost capacity to produce a rice crop in Haiti to feed those people because of what I did." [20]

From Food to Fuel

A similar worse-outcome resulted from the U.S. federal mandate to use biofuels in cars. As part of the 2007 U.S. Energy Independence and Security Act, the government stipulated the use of a certain amount of renewable fuels in transportation: 36 billion gallons by 2022.[21] This created a de facto market and a strong signal for industry to create plans for renewable energy for the long-term and reduce American dependence on oil.

The problem with this biofuel mandate, however, was that the supply chain for ethanol was not taken into account. When viewed holistically, the footprint for ethanol is worse than for oil. Furthermore, the artificial market for ethanol caused farms around the world to shift from growing food for people's mouths to growing biofuels for Americans' cars, contributing to higher food prices and food shortages. In addition, the United States limits how much of its corn crops can be used for fuel. These limits led to Brazilian farmers growing biofuels in Brazil and exporting them to the U.S., while the U.S. grew corn and shipped it to Brazil for food.[22] The impacts of these policies have been disastrous.

The lesson from these examples is not to stop taking action or stop being proactive. Rather, the lesson is to think through the possible second-order consequences of what we do before moving forward.

Optimism Bias

In addition to having a bias for action, humans have a tendency to be optimistic, expecting better outcomes without having sufficient evidence to support those expectations. For example, how many entrepreneurs embark on a business considering that it may fail, and how many new businesses actually succeed?

Because I've successfully founded and run a 150-person business, friends often seek my advice when wanting to start their own business. They naturally think I'm a risk-taker and will gladly encourage them to quit their jobs and take the entrepreneurial plunge. They often tell me that others support their decision to quit and strike out on their own.

So, they're very surprised when I tell them the harsh realities of running your own business. They're likewise surprised if I'm not supportive. But the truth is, most small businesses fail, regardless of the entrepreneur's enthusiasm. Would-be entrepreneurs need to know the real risks of operating a business. Friends sometimes encourage friends to make bad choices in the interests of being positive and polite. Don't do your friends or colleagues that disservice. Let them make an informed decision weighing the risks, pros, and cons.

Optimism bias shows up in all kinds of scenarios. People underestimate their chances of losing their job or being diagnosed with cancer, overestimate their lifespan, and envision themselves as achieving more than their peers.[23]

Optimism is a good thing, but blind optimism can lead to many unintended consequences.

The Perils of Not Making a Fuss

While humans generally tend toward action, with an optimistic eye, there are times when people fail to take action—even when they know they should.

In late January 1986, I was a junior at Ithaca College, sitting in a quantum physics class when the chairman of the physics department burst in and interrupted the class. The chairman told us that the Space Shuttle Challenger had just blown up. My professor's first response to the shocking news was: "That f***ing O-ring."

How did he know to blame the O-ring, long before the official investigation proved it was the cause? He knew because he had worked on the solid rocket booster at Cornell, which is near Ithaca College. Engineers had the capability to anticipate what could go wrong. He knew the O-rings were a weak link in the booster design and that cold weather made them stiff. So why did the Challenger take off that fateful morning?

The problem was groupthink. The pressure to conform and not rock the boat (and especially the bosses' boat) causes people to stifle their knowledge of unintended and harmful consequences. Psychological experiments have even shown that people will disbelieve their own eyes rather than give an answer different from the group's consensus. Add to that pressures to meet deadlines and stay within cost ceilings, and the unintended results can be tragic.

In 2001, the Pontiac Aztek was intended to be one of a new generation of innovative GM vehicles. GM wanted to combat criticism that its vehicles were too staid, so it tried something new and radical. Yet "new and radical" is not the same as "good" and the initial Aztek concept ranked dead last in Pontiac's early market research clinics.

But Don Hackworth, the leader of Pontiac's product development team, wasn't going to let negativity get in his way. He reportedly said, "I don't want any negative comments about this vehicle. None. Anybody who has bad opinions about it, I want them off the team."[24] At one level, the strong-willed management style worked well. The Aztek development project met all its internal goals and schedules. The trouble was, the result was nothing customers wanted.

The leader's edict about no negative comments meant no one voiced their opinion, much less their concerns. Yet the edict couldn't censor the automotive press or consumers when the vehicle went to dealers' showrooms. The vehicle was widely attacked from a design standpoint and received several designations as one of the "ugliest" cars built. Aztek's first-year sales were less than 15 percent of the volume Pontiac expected. Quite a few were dumped on middle managers and the rest sent to rental fleets.[25] Cheering may sound great inside an echo chamber and motivate people to work hard, but those sounds are likely to result in the creation of a product that fails on the world stage.

CONTRARY REACTIONS

Other quirks of human behavior can cause an equal and opposite reaction from the one intended. Whispering, for example, may work better than shouting to get people to be quiet and listen. Or consider the fact that when someone tries to suppress or censor something, that act of suppression itself tends to raise its profile. The bigger the secret is, the greater the curiosity. This phenomenon is also called the "Streisand effect."

Our Fascination With Forbidden Fruit

Beginning back in 2002, the California Coastal Records Project (CCRP) photographed the entire California coastline in an effort to document environmental changes through aerial photographs. The Malibu home of singer and actress Barbra Streisand happened to be in one of the photographs, and she sued the CCRP for invasion of privacy. The lawsuit drew attention from the press as being harmful to freedom of speech. Prior to the news story, the photo of Streisand's home had been downloaded only six times, two of which were by Streisand's lawyers. But as a result of the press coverage, the photograph of her home drew 420,000 visits in one month after the story broke.[26][27]

Although Streisand may not have known better, spy agencies should know creating a fuss is no way to keep things secret. But, on April 6, 2013, Wikimedia France issued a press release saying that France's homeland intelligence agency (the Direction Centrale du Renseignement Intérieur or DCRI) had demanded that Wikimedia take down an article on the French-language Wikipedia about a French military compound, saying the article contained classified military information. Wikimedia France asked which parts of the article should be deleted, explaining that the article was based on public information from a 2004 documentary made by a French television station in cooperation with the French Air Force. The DCRI refused to specify what should be removed and insisted the entire article be removed.

When Wikimedia did not comply, the DCRI summoned a Wikipedia volunteer to its offices and threatened him with arrest if he did not delete the article right then and there. He deleted it under protest, saying the deletion contravened the rules of Wikipedia. A Wikipedia colleague in Switzerland restored the deleted article, and Wikimedia ran its press release.

The DCRI's attempt to censor the page simply brought it worldwide attention. The page became the most-viewed page on French Wikipedia for a time, with 120,000 page views the weekend after the press release, and was subsequently translated into other languages.[28][29][30]

Risk Homeostasis: Safer Cars Create Riskier Drivers

Does safety equipment make people more reckless? Researchers Adam T. Pope and Robert D. Tollison of the Federal Reserve Bank of Kansas City found evidence that it does. Looking at NASCAR race data, they found that after NASCAR mandated head and neck restraints for drivers, there were more on-track accidents.[31]

Although we expect race car drivers to take risks, the same effect shows up in the more sedate world of suburban sedans. Research from the Massachusetts Institute of Technology (MIT) AgeLab found that risk of car accidents actually increased when a car was equipped with a collision avoidance system. In a different experiment, researchers asked volunteers to drive go-karts with and without seat belts. They found that the people wearing seat belts drove their karts faster.[32]

This phenomenon is called *risk homeostasis*, and it occurs when people adjust the riskiness of their behavior to compensate for the perceived riskiness of their environment in ways that the person thinks will equalize the total risk. The MIT research shows drivers change their behavior in response to technology. The drivers drove more aggressively because they believed that the warning system would protect them to a greater degree than it actually did. Similarly, adaptive cruise control that regulates the following distances between cars might enable people to follow more closely at higher speeds, thereby increasing their risk. Risk homeostasis combined with erroneous risk models explains why a safety-promoting technology can actually increase deaths and injuries.[33]

Risk homeostasis works in both directions. Increasing the riskiness of the environment reduces risky behavior. Dutch traffic engineers found a very clever way to reduce traffic accidents involving pedestrians and bicycles. Instead of adding more safety signs, more lane dividers, and more separation between types of traffic, they reduced them. They removed road markings, guard rails, traffic signals, formal crossings and curbs, even around school playgrounds. The result was a big drop in accidents in the years after they created these "Shared Space" traffic zones. "When a situation feels unsafe, people are more alert," according to a study of seven of these projects.[34]

The Shared Space approach to making roads safer by making them seem riskier does raise a key question of what consequences do we really want. "A lot of cyclists say they do feel unsafe," said Hans de Jong, a former Dutch government road safety engineer of these Shared Space traffic zones. "There is an argument that one shouldn't feel entirely safe," added Ben Hamilton-Baillie, a British urban architect. "There is a constant dilemma in this field; whether we are seeking improvements in perceptions of safety or improvements in actual safety."

So, what is the bottom line? Often, we have to accept the lesser of two evils. Almost every action provokes some kind of reaction. It may be true that wearing a seat belt leads us to feel safer and drive faster resulting in an unintended consequence. But it's also a matter of scale, or proportion. We may save 100,000 lives a year with safety belts while offsetting that with an additional 10,000 new deaths from faster driving. The net savings of 90,000 is still worth it.

Part 2

How Bad Can It Be?

5

FAILURE À LA MODE

Having been a Lean Six Sigma deployment leader earlier in my career and Master Black Belt, I'm partial to rigorous methodologies. Failure Mode and Effects Analysis (FMEA) is one such a technique. It's one off the tools you should have in your toolkit to minimize the chance of unintended consequences. If the devil is in the details, FMEA is a great way to trace the kind of mischief the devil might wreak.

Origin and Purpose

In the years after World War II, the aerospace industry took off with new jets and rockets, and planes and missiles going higher and faster. The industry underwent explosive growth. Unfortunately, a lot of those new jets and rockets were exploding, literally—the ultimate unintended consequence. The U.S. Army invented FMEA in 1947 to analyze design failures in aerospace projects. NASA subsequently used FMEA on numerous projects from Apollo onward, and the U.S. automotive industry has used it extensively, with majors like Ford Motor Co. publishing an FMEA Handbook. Today, it's used in nearly all industries, from healthcare to manufacturing to food service. FMEA can be used to avoid product design defects, deaths from medical errors, botched business process implementations, and other problems.

How to Use FMEA

FMEA has two parts that fit hand in glove. The Failure Mode (FM) part identifies what might go wrong, and the Effects Analysis (EA) part analyzes the consequences of those failure modes. Once you have the analysis, it's a matter of looking at ways to prevent the failure from happening or to mitigate the effects of that failure.

FMEA is best done by a cross-functional team, because team members from different departments (design, purchasing, engineering, sales, marketing, quality, customer service, etc.) have different experiences and perspectives. Each person may be aware of different types of failures or potential consequences of a failure. A consequence could be anything from a product appearing differently than intended to deaths from medical errors, a botched business process, or loss of a customer. Having a cross-functional team makes it more likely someone will notice something that others didn't.

The team should first define the purpose of the system they'll be analyzing: "What is the purpose of this system, design process or service? What do customers expect it to do?"[35] Starting with a clear definition of the purpose ensures the team scrutinizes failures that may have potentially significant consequences. For example, a company might be analyzing a proposed strategic growth initiative designed to expand the product range, the customer base, the frequency of purchase, or some other way of increasing company revenues. This step helps identify and forestall unintended outcomes, including discrepancies in the initiative's purpose.

Second, the team will usually break the system down into separate subsystems, parts, or process steps and identify the function of each part. Let's say the strategic growth initiative is trying to grow revenues by enlarging the company's product range. Key subsystems might include: the engineering group, which will develop the new products; the factory that will make the new products; the sales group; and the distribution arm of the company. A modular view helps in two ways: 1) It helps the team see the possible failure modes in each part of the system, and 2) it helps the team work through the consequences of a failure inside one part that causes problems in another part of the system.

Third, for each function, the team asks, "What are all the ways failure could happen?" The failure might be defects, wear and tear, maintenance issues, or even human error in using the product or process. Maybe the engineering team will take longer to develop the product than was planned, maybe the factory doesn't have the capacity to make the new products, maybe some of the new products will be too small or too big for the current warehouse, maybe the new products will simply cannibalize sales of the old ones. These are the *failure modes*.

Fourth, for each failure mode, the team identifies the consequences of this failure on the system, related systems, related processes, customers, and regulations. For the growth initiative example, the effects might include higher costs, service problems, customer dissatisfaction, or even a decline in revenues instead of an increase. These consequences are the "effects." For each effect, the team assigns a number (on a 1 to 10 scale) to each of three categories:

> 1. Severity (the more severe the effect's consequences are, the higher the number). For example, a minor delay in the new product launch might not be so bad, but a decline in revenue—the opposite of the desired effect—would be severe.

2. Probability of occurrence (the more likely it is to occur, the higher the number). For example, schedule overruns on new product development can be common, but maybe the probability of cannibalized sales is very low because the proposed new products are different from the company's old products.

3. Detection likelihood (the harder to detect before the customer is affected, the higher the number). For example, factory capacity issues should be easy to spot, but a decline in customer loyalty would take time to detect.

Fifth, the team multiplies those three numbers to get the Risk Priority Number (RPN). The team then uses the RPNs to prioritize which effects to focus on first. The higher the RPN, the greater the overall risk when taking a holistic view of severity, likelihood of occurrence, and ability to detect or mitigate the problem.

Finally, the team identifies actions that can be taken to mitigate the overall risk which can be accomplished by some combination of reduced severity and/or reduced likelihood and/or improved detection.

When to Use FMEA

FMEA is ideally suited to manufacturing because it promotes high reliability of products and faster product development times. But FMEA can also be used in the services industry. Carl S. Carlson, author of *Effective FMEAs: Achieving Safe, Reliable, and Economical Products and Processes Using Failure Mode and Effects Analysis*, advises using FMEA for:

- New technology.
- New designs where risk is a concern.
- New applications of existing technology.
- Potential for safety issues.
- History of significant field problems.
- Potential for important regulation issues.
- Mission-critical applications.[36][37]

In short, any time you're developing something new or making a change to an existing important process, FMEA can help you avoid unintended consequences.

6

THE POWER OF THE LAW

Some unintended consequences seem like rare or fluke events. A bad outcome may seem like just a "wrong place at the wrong time" accident. But sometimes the math on places and times lets us foresee (and avoid) these outcomes or make a sound risk-reward trade-off. Using the right kinds of statistics can help separate bad luck from bad decisions.

It's Not Easy to Think in Probabilities

Humans are wired to think in certainties. We want to know if the weekend will be sunny or not. If it is, we'll have a picnic. If it's not, we'll clean out the basement. We're bummed when the picnic gets rained out, and we're bummed if we're up to our eyeballs in junk while the sun is shining.

Unfortunately, we don't live in a world of certainties; we live in a world of probabilities. Sometimes stuff happens and sometimes it doesn't. But if you tell your boss there's an 80 percent chance of making a June deadline, the boss tends to "round the number up" to 100 percent in her head and seems surprised (and perhaps even angry) if the schedule slips. But 80 percent actually means there's a one in five chance of a problem. Given a lot of projects, one in five actually means the probability is high that some project will miss its deadline. Why are we surprised?

If a coin toss comes up heads five times in a row, do you bet on heads or tails on the next toss? Many people invoke the "law of averages," that if a coin has come up heads too many times in a row, it's bound to be tails pretty soon. And they're right. It IS likely to come up tails pretty soon, but no sooner than it is likely to come up heads again. Both are 50 percent likely, in fact. The law of averages says nothing about the next toss. It is always 50 percent.

The disconnect between intuition and fact grows even larger when we start thinking about consequences. Most people would say that a 1 percent chance of something being true means it isn't true. After all, 99 percent of the evidence says it is not true. But what if that slim 1 percent chance is tied to something important like the maintenance of an airliner's engines or the chance of weapons of mass destruction in an unstable country? It's one thing to take a chance on a soggy picnic. It's a different matter when many peoples' lives are at stake. Imagine if one in 100 planes fell from the sky. Would anyone fly?

Here Comes the Bigger One

How bad can things be? How good can things be? Sometimes the unintended consequence comes from the unexpected magnitude of the events. In those cases, history can often give us a good estimate: Prior results provide insight into likely future ones. The weights of the last thousand customers coming into a shop provide a pretty good estimate of the range of weights for the next thousand customers. The next customer to walk in the door won't be a 2,000-pound person. Many things in life and business follow the familiar bell curve or normal distribution, with most consequences being average, a few events being greater or less than average, and no events being crazy big or absurdly small. But life isn't always normal.

When the Tokyo Electric Power Co. (TEPCO) designed the Fukushima Daiichi nuclear reactor in 1966, the company was concerned about the risk of tsunamis. A careful review of historical records dating back to the year 1273 suggested the potential for no more than a 3-meter tsunami. Being extra cautious, TEPCO built a 5.7-meter high sea wall and built the reactor 10 meters above sea level.[38]

On March 11, 2011, however, the strongest earthquake ever to hit Japan in recorded history generated a 14-meter tsunami that inundated the reactor complex, disabled the cooling systems, and led to the meltdown of three of the six reactors. Ironically, in building the reactor, TEPCO intentionally removed two-thirds of a natural 35-meter high seaside cliff that could have protected the complex. The Fukushima reactor failed because tsunamis don't follow a normal distribution. In a 4.5-billion-year-old world, an 800-year history of tsunamis less than 3 meters was obviously no guarantee that a 14-meter one couldn't happen—or wouldn't.

The Science Behind the 80-20 Rule

This pattern, in which most tsunamis are small but a few are extremely big, is an example of a different kind of statistical phenomenon than the more friendly bell curve. It's related to the familiar 80-20 rule, or Pareto principle. In the 80-20 rule, 80 percent of the time spent on a project goes to 20 percent of the tasks; 80 percent of a company's profits come from 20 percent of its customers; 80 percent of the money goes to 20 percent of the people; and so forth. The 80-20 rule is about less-common events or things (the 20 percent) having extraordinary consequences or importance (the 80 percent).

Every year, seismologists detect about 1,300 strong earthquakes of magnitude 5 to 5.9 that are capable of causing damage. Seismologists also detect about 134 earthquakes of magnitude 6 to 6.9. These are much bigger quakes, with 10 times the shake amplitude, which equates to 32 times the destructive energy of those in the 5 to 5.9 range. But those quakes happen one-tenth as often (think about severity and likelihood of occurrence from Chapter 5's FMEA). Finally, seismologists record about 15 quakes of magnitude 7 to 7.9. These are another 32 times more energetic and approximately another one-tenth as likely. And, about once a year, a monster quake of magnitude 8 or higher happens.[39] For earthquakes and damage, the 80-20 rule is more like a 99-1 rule, with less than 1 percent of the big quakes causing more than 99 percent of the damage. This pattern in which the consequences multiply while the probabilities divide is known as a *power law*.

Power Laws Rule

Power laws rule in nature and the lives of people. Earthquakes, tsunamis, volcanoes, hurricanes, tornados, floods, landslides, and forest fires all follow power laws. Even the consequences of human aggression—such as terrorist activities, cybercrimes, and wars—generally follow a power law. Power laws aren't always about bad consequences. Power laws also affect positive consequences, such as the number of copies sold of bestselling books, the popularity of Internet sites, the sizes of cities, the sizes of oil reserves, people's wealth and income, and even the number of goals scored by the best soccer players.[40][41]

Power laws mean that freakishly large consequences can happen, but are extremely rare. People and companies should therefore be ready if things go viral and explode. But power laws also imply that lackluster or mundane consequences are, by far, the most frequent outcomes. Most high school football players don't make it into the NFL. Most musicians don't record a hit song. And most actors wait tables rather than wait to get their Academy Award.

"Well, I got 6 out of 7 days right this week!"

Learning From Near Misses

Although it seems like history provides a poor guide for things following a power law, that's not true. It's all in the interpretation of the historical data. A pattern of near misses or low-consequence events can tell you that extremely serious consequences *could* occur with some low frequency in the future. For example, if we see 100 minuscule events, 10 minor events, and one medium event, then it may be possible to infer that as the future progresses and we see more and more events, then eventually we get 1,000 minuscule events, 100 minor events, 10 medium events, and one major event.

It's been 25 years since the Loma Prieta earthquake struck the San Francisco Bay Area as a World Series game was about to start, making the disaster widely shared with the American people as TV crews turned the cameras toward the ravaged city.[42] The Bay Bridge was seriously damaged; fires broke out in the Marina District; dozens of people were killed and many more lost their homes. With the 25-year anniversary recently, many people were asking, "Could it happen again?"

Over the last 200 years there have been about a dozen earthquakes greater than 6.9 that hit California. That doesn't sound like a lot, but it amounts to about one per generation, or three to four per lifetime. Californians experience an estimated 37,000 tremors a year, with most of them being minor. Now scientists are predicting not just one big earthquake but a cluster of stronger earthquakes.[43]

Preparing for something that hasn't happened in decades is hard, but can we really ask "If?" another earthquake of that magnitude could happen again? Of course not. Instead it seems rather obvious that the only real sensible question to ask is "When?" followed by "How do we prepare?"

7

GAMES PEOPLE PLAY

Techniques like FMEA and power law analysis are great for thinking through the consequences associated with random phenomena like accidents and mechanistic things like a company's products. But a lot of unintended consequences occur when people enter into the picture. Too often, people don't behave the way we thought they would. Yet, in retrospect, people's *unexpected* behavior may not be surprising because people have choices of different actions in any given situation.

A Mortal Fear of Sick Patients

The state of New York tracks the outcomes of heart surgeries to rate the performance of heart surgeons. It then publishes the mortality rates of each surgeon, so that future heart patients can decide which surgeon to use. From the time tracking began more than 15 years ago, mortality rates have plummeted to just one-third of what they were. Proponents say that's because patients are selecting the best doctors, which pressures all doctors to improve their practices.[44]

A deeper look, however, reveals there is more than one way a doctor can improve his or her performance score. Besides practicing safer surgery procedures, surgeons can avoid operating on the sickest patients who are least likely to survive. Research by Karen E. Joynt, Ashish K. Jha, and their colleagues confirmed fewer surgeries were performed in regions that mandated public reporting of outcomes compared to regions that did not have those mandates. Luckily, in regions that have higher concentrations of hospitals (creating a competitive market), the results did suggest that a higher quality of care outweighs the effects of cherry-picking patients.[45]

The Choice Is Yours (and Theirs, Too)

Game theory is a way to think about choices—your choices and the choices made by others in reaction to the choices you might make. If you've ever played tic-tac-toe, then you've almost certainly used game theory to think about your moves: "If I put my X here, then my opponent puts their O there, then I can win by…."

The basics of game theory involve filling out a table of your choices and the other player's choices. For each combination of choices, the table has a score to reflect the advantages or disadvantages of the players picking that combination. Such a table makes it clearer which choice will work best for you given that the other player is thinking about their best choice, too. Game theory works for competitive situations, when two sides are looking for win-lose combinations of choices, as well as for cooperative situations, when two sides are looking for win-win combinations.

Consider, for example, the decision to advertise or not and whether your competitor is advertising. If your opponent is not advertising and you start advertising, you'll spend money on the campaign and grab some market share from them. That seems like a good idea. But then your competitor will probably decide to spend money and start advertising to regain their lost market share. Now you've inadvertently caused the competitive nature of your relationship to heat up. It's the same as two countries finding themselves in an arms race. One decides it will be better protected with bigger and better weapons—the other then follows suit. In the case of the advertising, both you and your competitor are spending money on advertising and both of you probably are back to having about the same market share you had before these expensive ad campaigns started. What seemed like a great idea has turned into something that costs money but doesn't change anything. Profits decline. Sometimes—inaction is the best action to take.

My point isn't that advertising is a bad idea. If consumers really didn't know about some key differentiator for your product, then advertising might work, even if the competitor starts advertising, too. That makes the payoffs of the moves and countermoves different.

Game theory provides a framework to lay out moves and countermoves, think about the outcomes from both points of view, and decide if your planned move is really a good idea given the likely countermove by your competitor. It's a great way to start thinking three steps ahead.

Move, Countermove, Counter-countermove

More complex games like chess or real life have a ramifying series of moves and countermoves. Each move changes the defensive and offensive options for future moves. Maybe you can open up the board to give yourself more freedom of movement. Maybe you can pin down your opponent's pieces so that they are more restricted. Or, you might create a poisoned pawn that entices your opponent to make a mistake. And, at the same time, your opponent is trying to do the same to you. The further ahead you think, the better.

When the Internet, e-commerce, and sites such as eBay rose to prominence in the late 1990s, UPS realized that the shipping industry was about to change, with more small businesses and individuals needing to ship things on a regular basis. UPS needed a retail presence to access these new markets. In 2001, UPS bought Mail Boxes Etc. and rebranded it as "The UPS Store." Of course, this sparked a countermove by FedEx, which then bought Kinko's and rebranded it "FedEx Office." Yet moving first gave UPS an advantage. UPS gained 4,000 retail outlets for an average of $46,000 each, whereas FedEx gained only 1,200 outlets and paid an average of $2,000,000 each.[46] And the game has not ended. Both delivery companies are fighting to offer new services, such as design and print, and to reach new markets such as opening outlets in hotel lobbies.[47][48]

An Open Mind for Open Games

For many games like tic-tac-toe, chess, or poker, each player's choices are defined by the rules of the game and don't change. There may be some chance

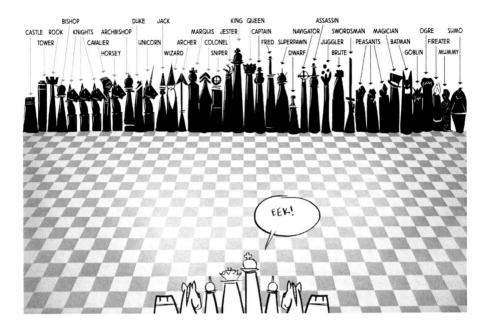

MEGA CHESS

involved with the deal of your hand or the roll of a die, but there is still a set of rules for what players can and cannot do. These are called *closed* games. But some games, like real life or business, lack predefined choices; they are fertile grounds for the fruits of human imagination and ripe for unintended consequences.

For example, when the British ruled India, they were alarmed by the number of poisonous snakes in Delhi. The government decided to offer a reward to anyone who brought in a dead cobra. Offering a bounty seemed like an efficient way to get rid of snakes without having to hire government workers to do the task.

At first, the policy worked well, but then enterprising people realized they could breed cobras, kill them, and bring them in for a reward. When the government realized what was happening, it ended the reward system. But when the program ended, the cobra farmers simply released their snakes, creating a net increase in the number of poisonous snakes. This "cobra effect" has happened again and again when bounties have been offered as a way to eliminate pests, including rats in Hanoi, Vietnam, and feral pigs in Fort Benning, Ga., as Stephen Dubner and Steve Levitt, authors of *Freakonomics*, document.[49]

When the British created their bounty for dead cobras, they assumed people would only choose between avoiding cobras versus catching and killing cobras. Given just those two choices, the bounty seemed like a great way to motivate people to catch cobras. That's what the British wanted, and they clearly did create a positive reward system for those who went out and caught cobras. What the British didn't expect was that people had a clever third choice.

Companies aren't immune to the cobra effect. When an Internet company offered a reward to its programmers for finding bugs in the software, it learned that some programmers were adding bugs in order to "find" them later and collect the reward. Thinking an additional step ahead allowed the company to outsmart those who had outsmarted the system. The company changed its policy and started giving programmers a bonus when no bug was found in code they had written, and it started paying a bounty to any customer who found a bug.[50]

Cat and Mouse: Which Will You Be?

We don't think about the alternative choices that others have because we're often too focused on assuming they will do what we want, or expect, them to do. A study of chess players found that one factor that distinguishes grand-masters from other chess players is that although the lesser-ranked players think many moves ahead, they tend to assume that their opponents will play the pattern they expect they will. Grandmasters, in contrast, look for ways the opponent might wreck their intended plan.[51]

Unintended consequences aren't usually the immediate outcome of a change but a series of unexpected outcomes. Therefore, anticipating unintended consequences means thinking ahead. You must be creative to imagine those things that haven't happened, may never happen, or that no one else has even considered.

The next section will give you the tools to think several moves ahead: using stories and narratives, scenario planning, systems thinking, and creativity to out-think your competition.

Part 3

What To Do About It

8

MANAGING UNINTENDED CONSEQUENCES

Unintended consequences happen. The world is complicated. Things go wrong. Our ability to predict the future accurately is far weaker than we think. The way to minimize the negative impact of unintended consequences—or to maximize their opportunity—is to think through the possibilities.

A great quote by French economic journalist Frederic Bastiat encapsulates this: "There is only one difference between a bad economist and a good one; the bad economist confines himself to the visible effect; the good economist takes into account both the effect that can be seen and those effects that must be *foreseen*." [52]

Here are three ways to see beyond visible effects.

1. Question the Numbers

In college I majored in math with a dual bachelor's in physics. I'm partial to numbers; but as a business person, let me tell you this: Numbers can give things a credibility they may not deserve. People make the mistake of thinking "the numbers say so, it must be true." Wrong. Numbers can be cherry-picked, massaged and arranged to support some of the craziest projects. Don't implement a project just because the cost-benefit analysis works. As Mark Twain once famously said, "There are lies, damn lies, and statistics."

Many unintended consequences are the result of a cost-reduction scheme that ends up increasing costs. Instead, look beyond the numbers: Do the underlying assumptions make sense? Are the numbers right? Where did the numbers come from? Who created the numbers? Do those people have incentives to bias the numbers? Are the creators of the numbers biased without knowing it?

"We could use a nine."

2. Consider Intangibles

When companies make the decision to go with the lowest-cost provider or the lowest-cost ingredient, they're saving money. It's a tangible benefit. But in doing so, they might miss the intangible costs, such as the cost to a brand's reputation if the product fails due to that low-cost part. If you examine the numbers on those costs, you might find the low-bid option has problems, such as poor workmanship, cut-rate materials, or a supplier on the verge of bankruptcy.

When apparel retailer Gap Inc. faltered in the 2000s, it brought in a new CEO who promised shareholders he would cut costs. That seemed to help the bottom line…until it led to insidious side effects. "'Finishes, washes, all the things that gave a garment more character—trims, sweater yarns,' were all switched to lower-cost alternatives, a former Gap designer said. 'If there were six things you used to do on a T-shirt, you'd do three or two.'" The company switched to cheaper fabrics and store cleanliness declined. With it, sales declined, forcing the company to slash prices.[53]

3. Experiment and Model

Sometimes the numbers are accurate, and no one can identify an unintended intangible. That doesn't mean the unintended consequence isn't hiding somewhere. *Experiments and models* are a good way to find those hidden consequences and test ideas before implementing them on a full scale. If you're going to battle the law of unintended consequences, it's a good idea to experiment first.

For example, growth of urban areas has been shown to increase the air temperatures. It's called the "heat island" effect. To combat the added heat in already-hot climates, experts suggested painting all the roofs white. The assumption was the white roofs would reflect light rather than absorbing it, thus reducing the surrounding temperatures more than the darker colors. Not surprisingly, that's exactly what happened. "We found that raising the reflectivity of buildings by painting their roofs white is an effective way of reducing higher average temperatures caused by urban expansion," said Matei Georgescu, an assistant professor in ASU's School of Geographical Sciences and Urban Planning.

The trouble was, the increased reflectivity also affected rainfall. Those dark buildings may have created a heat island effect, but the heat island created rising hot air that led to clouds and rain. In fact, Georgescu and his team found that painting roofs white led to a significant reduction in rainfall, which was not good news for the semi-arid environments in Arizona where this experiment was conducted.

In short, changing one thing may lead to unexpected changes in other things. It's better to try a small experiment first and then watch for the small unintended consequences. The logic that white roofs would reduce heat was unassailable and, in fact, correct. But the logic did not go far enough, and it's good that an experiment revealed the side effects. Experiments can catch repercussions before they spiral out of control.[54]

THE POSITIVES OF NEGATIVE THINKING

It's okay to think about all of the things that can go wrong. It doesn't make you a negative person. In fact, positive consequences can be gained from thinking about all of the negative things that can go wrong.

The Power of Stories

When George Buckley took over as CEO of 3M, about two months into his tenure, he gave a writing assignment to all business unit heads. He asked each executive to write a narrative, like a business school case, about the worst things that could happen to their business and how they would handle it. Buckley wanted a story, not PowerPoint slides. He didn't want the executives to delegate the task, because he wanted his business heads to understand the perils for themselves. Many executives had never written more than two to three pages before, but they did it for the new boss.

The following year, Buckley made them do it again, and by the third year the executives realized this crazy exercise wasn't going away. But by the fourth year, Buckley started getting feedback from some of the executives about how these narratives had saved their necks. The executives had always had growth plans, but they had never thought about risk in this manner before.[55] Writing a narrative about potential perils takes much more thought than simply listing bullet points. Bullet points tend to be shallow because they don't show the reasoning behind them or the relationships among them. Narratives, however, reveal your thinking and your assumptions. You have to explain your thoughts and can't be intellectually lazy.

For example, a typical strategic plan might call for growing market share by 20 percent, increasing profits by 25 percent and increasing the number of new product introductions to 15 a year. But how do those three objectives interconnect? How will they be achieved? What assumptions do they make? Are they mutually consistent?

Unlike listing bullet points, if executives have to tell a story—a strategic story—they need to set the stage describing the current as-is situation in terms of the industry's dynamics, economics, competitors, and forces driving change. Then, like any good story, the strategic story has a dramatic conflict: the challenges the company faces when trying to achieve its plans. Finally, the story ends with a resolution to the conflict, explaining how the company can overcome the challenges and succeed in meeting its goals.

Strategic stories expose flaws in thinking. They force executives to think about the negative things that might happen so they are not caught unaware. Finally, strategic stories inspire the company to execute the plan because, rather than just a bullet point, the plan is now a clear vision that inspires action.

STOIC PHILOSOPHY

Many people go through life without thinking about a guiding philosophy. Philosophies of life, such as Stoicism, concern themselves with daily life.[56] They teach us which things are most valuable and how best to attain them. In business, the tools in this book can help you implement a Stoic management philosophy.

A Happy Stoic Is Not an Oxymoron

In ancient Greece, Zeno formulated Stoicism around 300 B.C., and he would not recognize today's depiction of stoical as "seemingly indifferent to or unaffected by joy, grief, pleasure, or pain." Two millennia have mangled Zeno's original intent. Originally, Stoicism was a practical philosophy for promoting happiness rather than quiet suffering. The original Stoics weren't against all emotion—they were against negative emotions like anger and fear because those emotions obstructed happiness.

The Stoic philosophy is, in fact, all about providing a path to happiness. As Epictetus, a famous Stoic said, "There is only one way to happiness, and that is to cease worrying about things which are beyond the power of our will." Stoics therefore accept the world as it is, thereby becoming more relaxed and content.

David Galland, in "The New Stoics," explained: "[Stoics] were early on in identifying and understanding that there are aspects of life they have no control over. Once they accept they have no control over a thing, a practicing Stoic puts it out of his mind."[57]

The Stoic philosophy lives on in the form of things like the Serenity Prayer that's popular with 12-step self-improvement programs. The prayer asks for "the serenity to accept the things one cannot change, the courage to change the things one can, and the wisdom to know the difference." Systems theory, as we briefly discussed in Chapter 1 and will cover in more detail in Chapter 12, helps you see how things are connected and what you can and can't change.

Appreciate the Positive and Don't Obsess Over the Negative

For one thing, Stoics accept that they will someday die, so they don't worry about it. Second, Stoics realize that good things may end, so they take time to appreciate them. William Irvine, in *A Guide to the Good Life*, writes:

> "Offer a Stoic a glass of fine champagne, and he probably won't refuse it; as he drinks it, though, he might reflect on the possibility that this will be the last time he drinks champagne, a reflection, by the way, that will dramatically enhance his enjoyment of the moment. Then again, offer a Stoic a glass of water, and he might go through the same thought processes with the same result."[58]

Regretting what happened in the past, for example, doesn't change it. Getting angry that your incoming plane is delayed doesn't make it arrive earlier. Instead, a Stoic will focus on what he can do: Get an alternate flight? Use a different mode of transportation? Change the meeting time?

Game theory (Chapter 7) can help you see where you or others have the freedom to make a different move. Analyzing the payoff matrix will help you pick a move to make the best of a bad situation. Game theory also shows you if some outcomes are inevitable because of the patterns of moves and countermoves.

If none of those options are feasible, then it's an opportunity for a test: Can the stoic prevent the situation from disrupting his tranquility? Can he use it to practice a trait he hopes to embody, such as kindness or courage? With such reframing, negative situations become opportunities for personal triumphs. If you understand human behavior such as the bias for action (Chapter 3) or risk homeostasis (Chapter 4), you might be less upset when these phenomena occur.

"Well, he IS carrying on."

Logical Thinking vs. Emotional Reacting

I'm including this chapter on Stoicism in this book because Stoicism is a useful philosophy for managing and avoiding unintended consequences. The philosophy does not prescribe inaction, fatalism, or resigning oneself to one's fate. Rather, it provides a mental framework for identifying what you can't control so you focus on what you *can* do something about.

Too often, unintended consequences arise from a lack of foresight or from emotions that drive a knee-jerk response to a problem. For example, a person might fear flying and choose, instead, to drive—which is actually the far riskier form of transportation. A Stoic would take a dispassionate look at the data on flying versus driving and see that despite the visceral fear of handing over control to the pilot and hurtling through the air at 600 miles per hour while six miles above the earth, flying is the safer choice. Stoicism is a philosophy of action driven by thoughtful reason rather than blind emotions.

The Stoic philosophy also helps us see the difference between unintended and unavoidable consequences. Maybe the alternative flight will be delayed, too. Maybe driving to the meeting will encounter a construction zone. Maybe we can't get ahold of the meeting participants to change the time.

As Scottish poet Robert Burns once said, "The best laid plans of mice and men oft go awry."[59] An 80 percent chance of meeting a deadline or closing a deal is an 80 percent chance, not a 100 percent one. The 20 percent downside happens one-fifth of the time. Sometimes we just have to play the hand we're dealt, even if we wish we had a better one. Remember that power laws rule (Chapter 6), so a spectrum of outcomes might occur, including a nasty one. By using logic to better control the consequences we can control—and also accepting that we can't make everything perfect all the time—a Stoic channels his or her energy toward creating happiness rather than useless regret and anger.

Failure Mode and Effects Analysis (Chapter 5) may seem like it's focused on the negative, but it's really a tool for looking at which failures you might be able to control and which ones really matter. FMEA can help you prioritize problems so you don't waste emotional energy or your company's resources on the small stuff. By using logic to better control the consequences we can control—and also accepting that we can't make everything perfect all the time—a Stoic channels his or her energy toward creating happiness rather than useless regret and anger.

SCENARIO PLANNING

Scenario planning, and its little brother what-if analysis, are excellent strategic thinking tools that are well suited for anticipating (and avoiding) unexpected consequences.

Specifically, *what-if analysis*, as its name implies, refers to thinking through different possibilities. For example, *what if* fuel prices rise 30 percent (or drop 50 percent as happened at the end of 2014)? *What if* a major customer goes bankrupt? *What if* demand for our new product is 200 percent higher than our highest estimate? That last one is a good problem to have, but it is a problem nonetheless (often referred to as a "missed opportunity").

Scenario planning goes even a step further than what-if analysis. What-if analysis is good for thinking through how to respond to events that you can foresee might happen, but generally speaking asking "what if" is limited to thinking one step ahead. Scenario planning is a technique designed not to predict the future, but rather to stretch your thinking about potentially very different futures and their consequences; it is a tool designed to help you think three steps ahead.

From the Usual Projections to Unusual Possibilities

Royal Dutch Shell pioneered formal scenario planning in the late 1960s and early 1970s. A quartet of planners at the company—Arie de Geus, then head of Shell's strategic planning group, and Pierre Wack, Peter Schwartz, and Kees van der Heijden—developed the technique when they saw that most executives believed the oil business would continue on a path, "as usual." Such a belief was not surprising because up until 1973 the oil industry had the steadiest growth of all major industries. Shell's planners, however, speculated that business might not continue as usual, and they were having a hard time convincing executives to challenge their assumptions. There was certainly no guarantee that the future would be different than expected, but if it was, they wanted to be prepared. The planners employed their new scenario planning technique as a way to help change their executive team's mental models.[60] That turned out to be a prescient move, because the Arab Oil Embargo and the rise of environmentalism brought changes that few others had foreseen as even remote possibilities—and no others had prepared for. The oil business, indeed, did not continue as usual.

Scenario planning works because it involves creating plausible stories about the future using trends, uncertainty, creativity, and known drivers of the business. Scenarios are "data-driven stories" that look at the forces that might change the future.[61] Because they are stories, scenarios—like 3M's narratives—help expose flaws in logic. Moreover, stories feel real and let you enter and live in them, thinking through how you might realistically respond. Scenario planning can be very powerful not only in challenging assumptions, but also in understanding how your stakeholders (e.g., customers, suppliers, or employees) and competitors respond to a given scenario.

This critical thinking and analysis are key to thinking more than one step ahead.

Scenario Planning in Real Life

A necessary input of scenario planning is to start with a central question or focal issue. For example, in 2010, Cisco (with the help of Peter Schwartz's Global Business Network) developed a set of scenarios for use in its strategy planning process. Cisco's focal issues were: "What forces will shape the Internet between now and 2025?" and "How might the use of the Internet and IP networks evolve?"

After identifying this focal issue, Cisco planners interviewed the company's executives and managers as well as external thought leaders from different industries to poll their thoughts about the main forces that would influence the Internet in the coming years. The purpose of this step was to identify the main "Axes of Uncertainty"—the divergent directions that would have the biggest consequences on the focal issue. In Cisco's case, planners found three axes (which were bipolar): "Network Build-Out" (whether the global broadband network was limited or extensive), "Technological Progress" (whether other technologies showed incremental or breakthrough change), and "User Behavior" (whether people and organizations had constrained or unbridled use of the Internet).[62]

Once the critical uncertainties are determined along with an understanding of the business's driving factors and trends, the scenarios and scenario stories can be established. For example, Cisco came up with four scenarios: "Fluid Frontiers" (technological breakthroughs, extensive Internet use, but limited broadband network), "Insecure Growth" (extensive network, technological breakthroughs, but limited Internet use), "Short of the Promise" (extensive network, but incremental technological developments and limited Internet use), and "Bursting at the Seams" (extensive Internet use, but limited broadband network and incremental technological advances). Usually, each scenario is written as a story or description with enough richness that people can envision a different world and its consequences.

The true value, however, comes from the analysis and critical thinking about the implications, consequences, and other impacts of each scenario. Scenario planning lets a company think about the future, unencumbered by projections of the past. What would the company do differently in each of the different scenarios? Are there actions that work in most or all of the scenarios? Are there actions that work great in some scenarios but have tragic consequences in other scenarios? Can the company watch for telltale signs or indicators that will point toward one scenario or another coming true?

By thinking through these stories and how you might handle them, you'll be less likely to take actions that have unintended consequences and better equipped to shape the future instead of simply following it.

Once Upon a Time There Was a Good Scenario

A good scenario is like a good story of a faraway land. The story helps you think about living and operating under different circumstances so that you can spot unintended or unforeseen consequences. A great scenario entails many factors, but there are four tips necessary to keep in mind:

1. Scenarios should challenge your thinking and assumptions. Simply extrapolating trends from the present won't do that.

2. You want more than one scenario, because the future could evolve down very different paths. Two to four scenarios is a good number—enough to think about radically different alternatives but not so many as to be unwieldy.

3. Each scenario should be dramatically different from the others, to stretch your thinking the most.

4. Each scenario should be internally consistent, even if it's not consistent with today's world.

The point is not to pick the most likely scenario, but to imagine different scenarios and imagine the different consequences of those scenarios and the different actions that you would take if those possible futures came to pass. By accepting that both the destination and the path are not predictable, you can focus on preparedness and responsiveness.

Knowing that the future might shift qualitatively, you can watch for fluctuations and novel opportunities and threats. By imagining different scenarios, employees can think about the different ways the world could move. Analogously, a flock of birds does not forecast when a hawk will appear, but it knows how to watch for, and then respond to, the hawk scenario if it becomes a reality.

The bottom line on scenarios? They challenge your assumptions and open your mind to the unthinkable.

APPLY SYSTEMS THINKING

Our complex world is going to produce unintended consequences, but we're much more likely to anticipate the possibility of those consequences if we use a *systems thinking* approach. Peter Senge, a systems scientist and co-faculty at the New England Complex Systems Institute, describes systems thinking as "a discipline for seeing wholes. It is a framework for seeing interrelationships rather than things, for seeing patterns of change rather than static 'snapshots.' It is a set of general principles—distilled over the course of the twentieth century, spanning fields as diverse as the physical and social sciences, engineering, and management."[63]

We're Back to Loops Again

As I briefly described in Chapter 1, systems thinking can help us see positive and negative feedback loops. The tricky thing about systems is that there's often a delay in the consequences while something accumulates in the system. We don't see the unintended consequences of our actions immediately, which fools us into thinking we've chosen the right action. For example, we've been emitting greenhouse gases by burning fossil fuels directly (gasoline and fuel oil) and indirectly (using fossil fuels like coal to generate electricity) for a hundred years, but climate change didn't start to rear its ugly head until the last couple of decades. Once it starts, positive feedback loops amplify the effects, as the article, "Terrestrial Ecosystem Feedbacks to Global Climate Change" explains:

"In similar manner to past climatic and large-scale ecosystem changes, human-induced global warming is expected to cause a poleward shift of forest zones, and thus decrease the reflectivity of the Earth's surface, increase absorption of sunlight, and enhance rates of warming —a positive feedback.

"Warming and associated decreases in soil moisture may bring about an increased frequency of natural fires. The burning vegetation would pump even more CO_2 into the atmosphere—a positive feedback.

"Elevated concentrations of CO_2 have been shown to cause stunted plant transpiration, the process by which plants release water to the atmosphere. Transpiration normally acts to cool the surface; thus, the result could be even higher regional temperatures at the surface—a positive feedback (although the global implications of this are not entirely clear)."[64]

Positive feedback loops exist in business, too. CEO compensation is a positive feedback loop (as is compensation of actors and professional athletes). As more people get seven or even eight-figure compensation, it becomes easier for others to make similar requests, creating a positive feedback loop. Salary surveys of CEO compensation further feed the loop. If everyone expects to be paid more than average, the average will keep going up.

Look Out for Loops

The good news is that once we understand the concept of positive and negative feedback loops, we can be on the lookout for them, and we can devise ways to take advantage of them. For example, grocery chain Tesco pioneered a loyalty card program in the grocery industry. Customers signed up to get the card, which asked for their demographic information. Every time customers made purchases, they scanned the card and in return got discounts.[65]

Tesco got a rich set of data: Every single item that a customer bought was recorded, paired with their demographic information, and mined for insights about what shoppers really wanted. The better Tesco understands its customers, the more products and services it can offer to them; the more products and services customers buy, the more Tesco can know about its customers. In short, customer knowledge begets program expansion and loyalty; program expansion and loyalty, in turn, begets more customer knowledge. Today, every grocery chain has adopted a similar model.

"Just two degrees warmer and the heat will finally shut off."

From Pieces to Patterns

As Senge says, the benefit of systems thinking is to see the world not as isolated events but to be able to recognize longer-term patterns of change and the underlying structures producing those patterns. This has many practical applications. Without a systems approach, people often take piecemeal steps to solve a complex problem and may actually make the problem worse. Not understanding why their solution isn't working, they simply try to do it harder or more.

For example, if someone is in an overheated office building in the winter (assuming they can't turn the thermostat down), the natural inclination is to open a window.[66] But as soon as the temperature drops, the thermostat turns the heat back on full blast. It wastes energy and doesn't result in a cooler office.

In contrast, a systems thinker would look at the whole system: The thermostat turns the heat on when the temperature drops below a certain level. How can you fool the thermostat? One way is to put a small heater right under it. That will cause the thermostat to measure the air temperature higher than it actually is in the rest of the building, and it will turn the heat off. Adding heat to the system at the right point can be a way to make it cooler.

Using Information Instead of Force

Systems thinkers realize from the beginning that stable systems have built-in ways of resisting change. Instead of fighting the system with brute force, they study it carefully to find the negative feedback loops, how they work, and where they are vulnerable. Let's take another example: a light breeze is too weak to knock you off your bike, but if that breeze blew smoke or dust in your eyes, it might cause you to fall. The obstruction causes you to shut your eyes, which reduces the flow of information to your brain and disrupts your balance, even though the wind itself couldn't tip you over.

That's the power of systems thinking: Seeing interrelationships and patterns of change can help you make better decisions and anticipate otherwise unanticipated consequences.

13

USING CREATIVITY TO OUT-THINK YOUR COMPETITION

In business and life, competitors don't always stick to the finite set of responses we expect and prepare for. Competitors can be creative, too. That means you've got to be ready for competitive responses from unexpected directions. The story of Super Bowl XLVIII, the Seattle Seahawks versus the Denver Broncos, is a case in point.

Seahawks' Supremacy

Though Bronco fans may not want to hear it, the Seahawks executed one of the best game plans in Super Bowl history. Their win—well, trouncing—of the Broncos wasn't due to Bronco quarterback Peyton Manning's failure to live up to his best when it mattered most. Rather, it was due to the Seahawks systematically disassembling his every move. Before the game, the Seahawks' defensive coordinator, Dan Quinn, and the other Seahawks coaches, pored over hours and hours of Bronco game tapes.[67] The coaches had to devise a defensive strategy to stop the seemingly unstoppable Manning.

A close analysis of the Super Bowl shows the Seahawks focused on containing the Broncos' highly acclaimed short passing game. They let Manning have his short passes—he connected on 34 of 49 passes—but they made sure his passes stayed short.

The Seahawks didn't blitz Manning. They knew from history that such a strategy wouldn't work. During the 2013-2014 season, Manning had a stellar over-100 rating when he was blitzed. So the Seahawks tried a different tactic.

Here's how Kevin Clark, sports reporter for *The Wall Street Journal*, put it:

> *"On Denver's first third down of the game, Seattle sent only three pass rushers. The rest dropped into coverage. This is almost unheard of in the NFL. The play resulted in a short three-yard completion that forced a punt. In another critical instance, the Seahawks sent the standard four pass rushers—yet defensive end Cliff Avril got to Manning anyway, hitting his arm as he threw. Because linebacker Malcolm Smith wasn't blitzing, he was there to intercept the floating pass and return it for a backbreaking touchdown."* [68]

In play after play, Seattle's defense kept the play in front of them and thwarted Manning. They didn't play Manning's game; they changed the game.

That's the thing about unintended consequences. Many times we're caught by surprise because we do what we've always done and expect the same results. But smart competitors come up with game-changing moves.

Failure of Imagination

The commission investigating the terrorist attacks of 9/11 cited a "failure of imagination" that kept U.S. officials from understanding the al-Qaida threat.[69] Although it doesn't say so directly, the *9/11 Commission Report* pointed to the government's inability to "connect the dots." As the report says:

> 1. The CTC [Counterterrorism Center] did not analyze how an aircraft, hijacked or explosives-laden, might be used as a weapon. It did not perform this kind of analysis from the enemy's perspective ("red team" analysis), even though suicide terrorism had become a principal tactic of Middle Eastern terrorists. If it had done so, we believe such an analysis would soon have spotlighted a critical constraint for the terrorists— finding a suicide operative able to fly large jet aircraft. They had never done so before 9/11.

> 2. The CTC did not develop a set of telltale indicators for this method of attack. For example, one such indicator might be the discovery of possible terrorists pursuing flight training to fly large jet aircraft, or seeking to buy advanced flight simulators.

> 3. The CTC did not propose, and the intelligence community collection management process did not set, requirements to monitor such telltale indicators. Therefore the warning system was not looking for information such as the July 2001 FBI report of potential terrorist interest in various kinds of aircraft training in Arizona, or the August 2001 arrest of Zacarias Moussaoui because of his suspicious behavior in a Minnesota flight school. In late August, the Moussaoui arrest was briefed to the DCI and other top CIA officials under the heading "Islamic Extremist Learns to Fly." Because the system was not tuned to comprehend the potential significance of this information, the news had no effect on warning.[70]

The methods to avoid a surprise military or terrorist attack apply just as aptly to anticipating an unintended consequence: 1) think about how surprise attacks might be launched, 2) identify telltale indicators connected to the most dangerous possibilities, 3) where feasible, collect intelligence on these indicators, and 4) adopt defenses to deflect the most dangerous possibilities or at least trigger an earlier warning.

In my book, *One Dot, Two Dots, Get Some New Dots*, I talk a lot about curiosity: You've got to be passionately curious about what's new and different.[71] And then—and this is the key part—you have to take the next step to think through how it might affect your business. Just because something is *unlikely* to happen doesn't mean it's *impossible* to happen. The trick to not being caught by surprise is to not get stuck just thinking about the routine. Before 9/11, intelligence agencies were focusing on the "knowns," the routines and most likely scenarios: airplanes being destroyed *by* bombs, not airplanes being used *as* bombs.

14

THE KNIGHT'S MOVE

How can you anticipate something unintended or unprecedented? How can you expect the thing that no one ever expected to happen? How can you navigate the law of unintended consequences? The answer is simple: You have to think three steps ahead.

For many, the law of unintended consequences sounds ominous, like something too negative to consider because the results are out of our control. But nothing could be further from the truth. Unintended consequences are really just *unanticipated* consequences, which we can anticipate through a robust approach to strategic thinking. When we don't think three steps ahead, we're forfeiting the opportunity to manage the future.

There's no playbook for strategic thinking. Instead, we must familiarize ourselves with the many mental models, potential biases, and feedback systems that will make us better strategic thinkers. As you have seen in this book, there are many methods and tools to help you be more strategic in your thinking. There are also things we can do every day to build our ability to collect and process information.

One of the simplest things you can do is something every child already knows: Be imaginative. Be on the lookout for new things and investigate them. Don't simply explore sources that conform to your preconceptions. You have to be able to imagine possible alternatives to your existing world, such as your competitors making choices that you wouldn't or couldn't make. As Larry Bossidy and Ram Charan said in their book, *Confronting Reality*, leadership today demands "unprecedented awareness of a greater range of external realities than ever before."[72]

Be curious. Pay attention to what your intuition tells you is interesting. Your intuition is really the sum of your experience. You may not be able to articulate why something caught your attention, but if it did, go with it. Trust yourself. Follow it up. Investigate it. Create scenarios around it. Ask: What might this look like if it continues to develop? What threat or opportunity does it pose to what we're doing now? The curious and the aware are always gathering information and asking questions. They are voracious dot collectors.

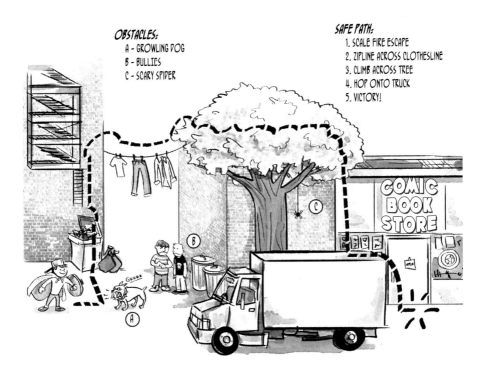

In my last book, *Become an Elite Mental Athlete*[73], I also talked about the importance of things like sleep, exercise, and nutrition to ensure our minds are primed to do the best strategic thinking possible. Raising your mental game—your cognitive acuity—allows you to better recall the things you've learned about thinking three steps ahead. Cognitive acuity also enables you to think more abstractly, seeing how your situation is more like another you've seen or read about elsewhere in an entirely different context. Recognizing how two seemingly different scenarios are actually alike means you can learn from the experiences of others, as well as broaden your ability to learn from your own experiences. You can better anticipate how your situation might play out—and why—when you can compare it to events that have come before.

In the end, thinking strategically is an innate skill, but there's no indication that it's one we are born with. Instead it's a skill we develop over time—over the course of our lives. The more you know about how to think three steps ahead and the more you practice it, the better you'll become.

When I first started playing chess with my father, I approached the game linearly. That's how my 9-year-old plays, too. She thinks: "If I move here, then Dad moves there, then I take Dad's queen and he takes my bishop…"

For a 9-year-old, that's impressive. But what she doesn't always remember is that once she makes a move, the next move I make might not be the one she anticipated. She's not yet thinking that beyond the first move there are many possible second moves that open up even more possibilities on the third move. Even when only looking three steps ahead, the number of combinations and permutations are growing fast. In fact they're growing exponentially. That can be frustrating for a child trying to learn chess.

Here's the upside: Remember earlier when we talked about which game was the easiest to win? That's right: chess. It's the most challenging game to learn but the easiest to win, and the winners are those who can see the greatest number of permutations on the board—combinations of moves and countermoves.

So don't make the mistake of only taking one step forward—you need to look two and three steps ahead. And you need to look around corners, too. You need to anticipate that your move might cause me to change my move. And you need to be able to make an unexpected "knight's move" that jumps into a new space. Knights are the only piece in chess that can jump other pieces and they give us great insight into how to think about different situations.

The bottom line? You don't need to *know* what's coming next—you've just got to be able to *imagine* what might come next. That's how you stay three steps ahead.

Sources

1   Yossi Sheffi, *The Resilient Enterprise,* MIT Press, 2007

2   "Aspirin Heart Warning," BBC News, Feb. 15, 2001, http://news.bbc.co.uk/1/hi/health/1168850.stm

3   Bridget Anderson, "The Philippine Snail Disaster," *The Ecologist*, March/April 1993, Vol. 23, No. 2, http://exacteditions.theecologist.org/read/ecologist/vol-23-no-2-march-april-1993-6495/32/3

4   "Systems Thinking," http://www.systemsthinker.com/interests/systems thinking

5   Andrew O'Connell, "Decreased Congestion in Beijing Undermines Air-Pollution Efforts," *Harvard Business Review*, April 29, 2014, http://blogs.hbr.org/2014/04/faster-traffic-in-beijing-undermines-air-pollution-efforts

6   Lucas W. Davis, "The Effect of Driving Restrictions on Air Quality in Mexico City," *Journal of Political Economy*, Vol. 116, Issue 1, 38-81

7   Grumpy Cat Limited, http://www.grumpycats.com

8   Robert K. Merton, *On Social Structure and Science*, The University of Chicago Press, 1996

9   Robert K. Merton, "The Unanticipated Consequences of Purposive Social Action," *American Sociological Review*, December 1936, Vol. 1, Issue 6, 894-904 http://www.d.umn.edu/cla/faculty/jhamlin/4111/2111-home/CD/TheoryClass/Readings/MertonSocialAction.pdf

10 Stephen J. Pyne, *Introduction to Wildland Fire: Fire Management in the United States,* John Wiley & Sons, 1984

Sources • • • • • • • • • • • • • • • • • •

11   "Australian Government Policy on Cane Toads," Australian Government, Department of the Environment, http://www.environment.gov.au/ biodiversity/invasive-species/publications/cane-toad-policy

12   "Cane Toad Invasion," http://www.canetoadsinoz.com/invasion.html

13   Claire Moodie, "Cane Toads Continue Destructive Path Across Australia," Australian Broadcasting Corp., April 15, 2014, http://www.abc.net. au/7.30/content/2014/s3986333.htm

14   "Theobald Mathew (Temperance Reformer)," https://www.princeton. edu/~achaney/tmve/wiki100k/docs/Theobald_Mathew_(temperance_ reformer).html

15   "Etheromaniac," http://www.worldwidewords.org/weirdwords/ww-eth1. htm

16   Bill Grantham, "Craic in a Box: Commodifying and Exporting the Irish Pub," *Cultural Adaptation*, edited by Albert Moran and Michael Keane, Routledge, Sept. 13, 2013

17   Ronny Frith, "Preventing and Avoiding Loopholes and Unintended Consequences in Legislation," National Conference of State Legislatures: Legal Services Staff Section Professional Development Seminar, Oct. 11, 2012, http://www.ncsl.org/documents/LSSS/SpotLoophole1.pdf

18   Jonathan Katz, "With Cheap Food Imports, Haiti Can't Feed Itself," *Huffington Post*, May 20, 2010, http://www.huffingtonpost. com/2010/03/20/with-cheap-food-imports-h_n_507228.html

19   "Feeding Haiti: A New Menu," *The Economist*, June 22, 2013, http://www. economist.com/news/americas/21579875-government-tries-load-up- plates-poorest-people-americas-new-menu

Sources

20 Maura O'Connor, "Subsidizing Starvation," *Foreign Policy*, Jan. 11, 2013, http://www.foreignpolicy.com/articles/2013/01/11/subsidizing_starvation

21 "Renewable Fuel Standard," US Environmental Protection Agency, http://www.epa.gov/otaq/fuels/renewablefuels

22 "From 1st- to 2nd-Generation Biofuel Technologies," International Energy Agency, November 2008, http://task39.org/files/2013/05/From-1st-to-2nd-generation-biofuel-technologies.pdf

23 Tali Sharot, "Optimism Bias: Human Brain May Be Hardwired for Hope," *Time*, May 28, 2011, http://content.time.com/time/health/article/0,8599,2074067,00.html

24 Bob Lutz, "How Bad Cars Happen: The Pontiac Aztek Debacle," *Road and Track*, Oct. 10, 2014, http://www.roadandtrack.com/car-culture/a6357/bob-lutz-tells-the-inside-story-of-the-pontiac-aztek-debacle

25 Andrew Dederer, "In Defense of: The Pontiac Aztek," *The Truth About Cars*, Oct. 25, 2006, http://www.thetruthaboutcars.com/2006/10/in-praise-of-the-pontiac-aztek

26 Mario Cacciottolo, "The Streisand Effect: When Censorship Backfires," *BBC News*, June 15, 2012, http://www.bbc.com/news/uk-18458567

27 "What Is the Streisand Effect?" *The Economist*, April 15, 2013, http://www.economist.com/blogs/economist-explains/2013/04/economist-explains-what-streisand-effect

28 "French Homeland Intelligence Threatens a Volunteer Sysop to Delete a Wikipedia Article," Wikimedia, April 6, 2013, http://blog.wikimedia.fr/dcri-threat-a-sysop-to-delete-a-wikipedia-article-5493

29 "Pierre-sur-Haute Military Radio Station," http://en.wikipedia.org/wiki/Pierre-sur-Haute_military_radio_station

Sources • • • • • • • • • • • • • • • • • • •

30   Kim Willsher, "French Secret Service Accused of Censorship Over Wikipedia Page," *The Guardian*, April 7, 2013, http://www.theguardian.com/world/2013/apr/07/french-secret-service-wikipedia-page

31   Adam T. Pope and Robert D. Tollison, "Rubbin' Is Racin': Evidence of the Peltzman Effect From NASCAR," *Public Choice*, March 2010, Vol. 142, Issue 3-4 March 2010, 507-513, http://link.springer.com/article/10.1007%2Fs11127-009-9548-2

32   Linda Gorman and Dwight Filley, "Mandatory Seat Belt Laws Cause Dangerous Driving, and Invade Privacy," Independence Institute, http://liberty.i2i.org/1999/02/10/mandatory-seat-belt-laws-cause-dangerous-driving-and-invade-privacy

33   "New Transport Technology for Older People: An OECD – MIT International Symposium," Cambridge, Mass., Sept. 23-24, 2003, http://www.oecd.org/sti/transport/roadtransportresearch/23725911.pdf

34   "'Riskier' Streets Reduce Accidents," Open Knowledge, April 16, 2012, http://knowledge.allianz.com/mobility/transportation_safety/?1841/risker-streets-reduce-accidents

35   Nancy R. Tague, *The Quality Toolbox*, Second Edition, ASQ Quality Press, 2005, 236–240

36   Carl S. Carlson, *Effective FMEAs: Achieving Safe, Reliable, and Economical Products and Processes Using Failure Mode and Effects Analysis*, Wiley, 2012

37   Carl S. Carlson, "Lessons Learned for Effective FMEAs," 2012 Reliability and Maintainability Symposium, January 2012, http://www.reliasoft.com/pubs/2012_RAMS_lessons_learned_for_effective_fmeas.pdf

38   Chester Dawson and Yuka Hayashi, "Fatal Move Exposed Japan Plant," *The Wall Street Journal*, July 12, 2011, http://online.wsj.com/news/articles/SB10001424052702303982504576425312941820794

Sources

39 "Earthquake Facts and Statistics," U.S. Geological Survey, http://earthquake.usgs.gov/earthquakes/eqarchives/year/eqstats.php

40 "Power Laws and Goal Scoring," *Soccer Statistically*, Jan. 20, 2013, http://www.soccerstatistically.com/blog/2013/1/20/power-laws-and-goal-scoring.html

41 "Power-Law Distributions in Empirical Data," http://tuvalu.santafe.edu/~aaronc/powerlaws/data.htm

42 Becky Oskin, "25 Years After Loma Prieta, Earthquake Science Is Transformed," *Live Science*, Oct. 17, 2014, http://www.livescience.com/48332-loma-prieta-earthquake-25th-anniversary.html

43 Brian Clark Howard, "Stronger Earthquakes Predicted for Bay Area—and They Could Come Soon," *National Geographic*, Oct. 13, 2014, http://news.nationalgeographic.com/news/2014/10/141013-bay-area-earthquakes-seismology-prediction-science

44 Bill Gardner, "The Unintended Consequences of Public Reporting of Mortality Outcomes," *The Incidental Economist*," March 4, 2014, http://theincidentaleconomist.com/wordpress/the-unintended-consequences-of-public-reporting-of-mortality-outcomes

45 Karen E. Joynt, Daniel M. Blumenthal, E. John Orav, Frederic S. Resnic and Ashish K. Jha, "Association of Public Reporting for Percutaneous Coronary Intervention With Utilization and Outcomes Among Medicare Beneficiaries With Acute Myocardial Infarction," *The Journal of the American Medical Association*, Oct. 10, 2012, Vol. 308, No. 14, http://jama.jamanetwork.com/article.aspx?articleid=1377923

46 Arik Johnson, "FedEx Acquiring Kinko's to Compete with UPS and Mail Boxes Etc. Stores," *Competitive Intelligence*, http://www.aurorawdc.com/ci/000094.html

Sources • • • • • • • • • • • • • • • • • • •

47 Patrick Henry, "Would-Be Printing Giants FedEx and UPS Slug It Out—But for What?" *What They Think*, Sept. 24, 2009, http://whattheythink.com/articles/53275-would-be-printing-giants-fedex-and-ups-slug-it-outbut-for-what

48 Barbara De Lollis, "UPS Store and FedEx Office Race to Open Hotel Locations," *USA Today*, Dec. 22, 2009

49 Stephen Dubner and Steve Levitt, "The Cobra Effect," Freakonomics Radio, Season 4, Episode 4, http://freakonomics.com/2013/10/24/the-cobra-effect

50 Joan Rigdon, "Netscape Is Putting a Price on the Head of Any Big Bug Found in Web Browser," *The Wall Street Journal*, Oct. 11, 1995

51 Mark Peplow, "Science Secret of Grandmasters Revealed," Nature, Aug. 6, 2004, http://www.nature.com/news/2004/040802/full/news040802-19.html

52 Frederic Bastiat, "What Is Seen and What Is Not Seen," Library of Economics and Liberty, http://www.econlib.org/library/Bastiat/basEss1.html

53 Stephanie Clifford, "A Humbled Gap Tries a Fresh Coat of Pep," *The New York Times*, April 28, 2012, http://www.nytimes.com/2012/04/29/business/a-humbled-gap-tries-a-fresh-coat-of-pep.html

54 Anthony Watts, "Law of Unintended Consequences Bites the 'White Roof UHI Solution' – Causes Reduced Rainfall," Arizona State University, Sept. 7, 2012, http://wattsupwiththat.com/2012/09/07/law-of-unintended-consequences-bites-the-white-roof-uhi-solution-causes-reduced-rainfall

55 Gordon Shaw, Robert Brown and Philip Bromiley, "Strategic Stories: How 3M Is Rewriting Business Planning," *Harvard Business Review*, May 1998, http://hbr.org/1998/05/strategic-stories-how-3m-is-rewriting-business-planning/ar/5

Sources

56 William B. Irvine, "Twenty-First Century Stoic," Oct. 27, 2010, http://boingboing.net/2010/10/27/twenty-first-century-2.html

57 David Galland, "The New Stoics," Casey Research, Sept. 28, 2012, http://www.caseyresearch.com/free-publications/caseys-daily-dispatch?ppref=JMD022EM1012A

58 William Irvine, *A Guide to the Good Life: The Ancient Art of Stoic Joy*, Oxford University Press, 2008

59 Robert Burns, "To A Mouse, On Turning Her Up in Her Nest With the Plough," http://www.robertburns.org/works/75.shtml

60 Pierre Wack, "Scenarios: Uncharted Waters Ahead," *Harvard Business Review*, September 1985, http://hbr.org/1985/09/scenarios-uncharted-waters-ahead

61 Peter Schwartz, "Winning in an Uncertain Future Through Scenario Planning," Delivering Tomorrow, Feb. 27, 2012, http://www.delivering-tomorrow.com/winning-in-an-uncertain-future-through-scenario-planning

62 *Scenario Planning for Freight Transportation Infrastructure Investment*, Transportation Research Board, National Cooperative Highway Research Program, Report 750, 2013, http://onlinepubs.trb.org/onlinepubs/nchrp/nchrp_rpt_750v1.pdf

63 Peter Senge, *The Fifth Discipline: The Art and Practice of the Learning Organization*, Doubleday, 1990

64 Daniel A. Lashof, Benjamin J. Deangelo, Scott R. Saleska and John Harte, "Terrestrial Ecosystem Feedbacks to Global Climate Change," *Annual Review of Energy and the Environment*, November 1997, Vol. 22, 75-118

65 Sandra Zoratti and Lee Gallagher, *Precision Marketing: Maximizing Revenue Through Relevance*, Kogan Page, 2012

Sources • • • • • • • • • • • • • • • •

66   Draper L. Kauffman, *Systems One: An Introduction to Systems Thinking*, Pegasus Communications, 1980

67   Brendan Prunty, "Super Bowl 2014: How Seahawks Defense Discovered and Exploited Peyton Manning's Tell," *The Star-Ledger*, Feb. 2, 2014 http://www.nj.com/super-bowl/index.ssf/2014/02/super_bowl_2014_seahawks_defense.html

68   Kevin Clark, "How the Seattle Seahawks Solved Peyton Manning," *The Wall Street Journal*, Feb. 3, 2014, http://online.wsj.com/news/articles/SB10001424052702304851104579361111580572276

69   "9/11 Panel Report: 'We Must Act,'" CNN, Friday, July 23, 2004, http://www.cnn.com/2004/ALLPOLITICS/07/22/911.report

70   "Foresight—and Hindsight," *The 9/11 Commission Report*, July 22, 2004, http://www.9-11commission.gov/report/911Report_Ch11.pdf

71   David Silverstein, *One Dot, Two Dots, Get Some New Dots*, Breakthrough Performance Press, 2012

72   Larry Bossidy and Ram Charan, Confronting Reality, Random House Business, 2004

73   David Silverstein, *Become an Elite Mental Athlete*, Breakthrough Performance Press, 2014